> "All the paths
> of the Lord are
> love and faithfulness."
>
> (Psalm 25:9)

We were at the Lambeth conference too! 150 ECUSA spouses of bishops were among the 650 Anglican spouses this summer in Canterbury. We spent three weeks immersed in the unique experience of being a global Christian Communion. Because of this experience, we have observations and insights on what it means to be the wider church. Thanks to Forward Movement Publications, the reflections of 33 spouses can now be heard and be one of the ways that we know who we are and can be as the Anglican Communion.

For the first time, the voices of bishops' spouses have been taken seriously as a membership. We have a unique and intimate view of how we live, pray and behave together. We are not only observers but participants. At Lambeth we gave ourselves over to be shaped by the Spirit as she moved among us. Because of the validity of what we experienced in Canterbury, our reflections now belong to the continuing discourse about the nature and future of our Anglican Church. Indeed, I believe that underlying these stories lies a deep and as yet untapped theology about the nature of God and God's will for our Communion.

We have chosen as the theme for this collection the image of "path," perhaps because we spent so much time walking! But the bedrock on which that metaphor rests is found in the observations of the spouses: that growth and transformation comes from staying at the table or Bible study together, accepting and honoring the uniqueness of each person. We found the strength to do this because of our profound trust and hope that through the encounters with God in scripture we could delight in difference. The blossoming of "love and faithfulness" were the signposts along the paths to tell us we were indeed on God's way.

The following words are drawn from the experiences of ECUSA Bishops' spouses submitted for this work. Interspersed into the body of this discription are questions raised by spouses themselves. It is our hope that these questions will allow readers to pause and reflect on their own reactions to our observations and their learnings of Lambeth.

My sincere thanks to all the bishops' spouses who contributed to this edition and to Sally Sedgwick from Forward Movement Publications. A special thanks to Joanne Skidmore who started us all down this path and who faithfully and lovingly accompanied this work to the end.

—Phoebe W. Griswold

Why a booklet of Episcopal Church in the United States (ECUSA) spouses' Lambeth stories connected with each other by way of a path? It is simply this: people have been anxious, delighted, hungry, enthusiastic, fascinated to hear the *stories* of Lambeth! What went on, what was it like to be there, to connect with others from around the Anglican Communion? It is in stories that we can bring others to the intricate tapestry of experience and journey that Lambeth was for those of us who were able to be part of this event. We are finding that people want to hear the stories that connect them to our greater communion. They love the details of issues, arguments, food, dress, programs, worship, and relationships. People are reminding us by their interest and enthusiasm that there is joy and excitement in being part of our diverse communion. We realize now that when we were at Lambeth, our people were there with us.

This is but one way to bring the Lambeth experience back to our people, to bring to greater life and understanding who we are as Anglicans from around the world.

The Lambeth experience has also been described by some as a kaleidoscope! A kaleidoscope is an instrument containing loose colored glass bits that are reflected in an endless variety of changing patterns and scenes. Just as one thinks one has the whole picture, it is profoundly changed with just a simple tilt of the wrist or twist of the neck, never to be quite the same again. Lambeth was like that and continues to be like that as we attempt to define it or describe it. The impressions are very vivid and colorful and filled with dynamic energy, but they are also elusive and hard to capture. They dance around in one's head and heart and spirit. There is no one story or incident, no single journey of Lambeth that can capture it, rather we hope to provide you a kaleidoscope, a collage of ever-changing and brilliant gems.

> Our hope is to produce an encounter for readers that interweaves the Lambeth stories of ECUSA spouses in a way that creates a doorway to the Anglican Communion and its ways of being church. We believe what will be seen through this doorway will be the transformative power of Bible study and the encountering of others who differ from us. It is in this witness to the work of the Holy Spirit that others may be moved to a deeper appreciation and understanding of the ways that we are drawn into, and become engaged in, God's plan for us, our communion, and our world.

What is Lambeth?

Since 1867, Lambeth Conferences have played a key role in the Anglican Communion's sense of historic continuity. Every ten years Anglican bishops from around the globe have gathered at the invitation of the Archbishop of Canterbury for a Lambeth Conference. From the first conference with 76 bishops, it has grown to one with nearly 800 bishops in attendance. At first, the gatherings were held at Lambeth Palace, but as the communion expanded, Lambeth Conference outgrew the Palace. It is now held in Canterbury, at the University of Kent, situated on a hill overlooking Canterbury Cathedral. There bishops and their spouses (who have been included the last two conferences) are housed in student housing and fed in dorm cafeterias.

Lambeth is seen as a time for the bishops to draw together to talk and worship, pray and confer, for conversation and formation. It is only through Lambeth gatherings that many bishops have an opportunity to meet with other bishops, especially with bishops from the far reaches of the communion. While not a legislative meeting, a Lambeth Conference can have wide-ranging importance through the advisory statements it adopts or the reports it issues.

The conference's greatest influence, however, may come simply through the effects of dialogue and debate among the bishops of vastly different experiences. At its best, a Lambeth Conference offers a purple-tinted lens to focus the issues and concerns of a far-flung church, producing an historic snapshot of the Anglican Communion's shifting and varied reality. "I think everyone who goes to Lambeth is changed by it, and hopefully they come away with a broadened sense of how Christ shows up in different parts of the world, in different guises, speaking different languages, appropriating different cultural realities." This is the perspective of Presiding Bishop Frank Griswold of ECUSA.

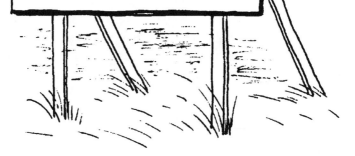

Lambeth
1998

There it was at last, the sign which we had been eager to see for months, THE UNIVERSITY OF KENT, and down the road a bit, "Welcome Lambeth Conference." Adventures were about to begin!

The 1998 Lambeth Conference was by far the most diverse gathering, reflecting the dramatic shifts in the communion's demographics over the past ten years. More than ten million Anglicans have been added to church rolls in the past decade, and most of this growth has been in the African provinces of Kenya, Nigeria, Tanzania and Uganda. All seven of the communion's newest provinces founded since the last Lambeth have been in second and third world countries. The phenomenal growth in African churches meant more faces of color in the ranks of bishops and spouses, with the most dramatic increase being in the Church of Sudan which went from four dioceses to 24, despite the turmoil of civil war and government-led persecution. It was also the first Lambeth with women bishops and male bishops' spouses. There were 10 female bishops with five spouses participating, four of them from ECUSA.

One ECUSA male spouse was most often asked, "What was it like being a minority among all those women spouses?" His response, "I had a high old time." Whether it was rehearsing in the play as the only male member of the cast or visiting the Old Canterbury Palace as the only male guest of Mrs. Carey that evening, "I felt right at home."

As an ECUSA male spouse I found that I was warmly received and welcomed by other spouses. There was not an over-curious wonderment or anxiety, but a feeling of inclusiveness on the part of the many spouses I met. They truly made me feel a part of the "family." We discovered that we shared many of the same concerns about ministry.

For most who attended Lambeth, bishops, spouses, visitors, staff, workers, it seems as if the stories they heard and experienced are what they carried away more than anything else. In Lambeth they encountered people from around the world, people who spoke the same language and others who spoke different languages. There were wide differences in skin color and in dress. There were bishops in purple and those who wore white and those who wore "native attire." There was much singing and even some swaying to the music, and a few Anglicans even moved into the aisle and danced.

Yet, it wasn't an easy time; there were difficult moments. There were hours in hot sweaty rooms that were small, packed, and where no air seemed to move. There were long walks across campus and long queues for meals. There were long waits at the portable loos (bathrooms), but they were wonderful loos; they had a plushness befitting a fine hotel with the added benefit of piped classical music.

Lambeth was like going away to college. We lived in "fellowship" with other bishops and spouses in college apartments or dorms and we walked miles upon miles to classes, sessions, seminars, Bible study, and other events. We got up early for Eucharist and stayed up late talking with those whom we shared living quarters. Like college, we were surrounded by learning experiences.

Technology was different from what most of us had remembered from our own college days. Every bishop had e-mail service and access to computers throughout the campus, making it possible for many bishops to stay-in-charge of things in their dioceses while at Lambeth. For some, having e-mail would be a new experience and for some, it seemed that there was no one back in the diocese who could receive their e-mail. There was instant translation into six different languages for almost all services, sessions and seminars. There were also telecasts to other parts of campus and video tapes of most sessions, so no one had to miss any sessions.

Lambeth was a lovely recipe for a sumptuous Anglican pie. Take a large group of church leaders of one religion and denomination from throughout the world, add a few of their spouses and others till you reach about 2,000 people. Stir in a variety of issues, marinate for three weeks in an unusually warm Canterbury, and behold, an Anglican pie.

On reflection, parts of that pie were delicious, other parts bitter and unpleasant, with each person's tastes varying significantly at times. Yet all of the Anglican pie was fascinating. With all the right ingredients present, why wasn't the taste of the pie more even? Could it have been that not all of the church leaders were from the same soil? That is, it could have been that because Christianity is safe and comfortable in certain parts of the world the taste and texture is different. Sometimes a wonderful sounding recipe just doesn't work in practice and needs to be tweaked a bit to improve it. To mix folk from all over the globe in the same small living space without thought to their cultural practices is a recipe for a not so even pie. Certainly we all learned a little bit about one another's cultures in those three weeks and it is true we were all Anglicans, but learning about each other the way we did was bumpy at best.

US citizens are usually open and honest and trusting. We desperately want to be liked by others and our expectation is we will be liked. Imagine being looked at with unpalatable hatred by a beautiful Sudanese woman, or ridiculed because we have no colorful national dress or mocked because we worry about relationships. We were told we should worry if we would still be alive next year, next month or next week. This is heavy stuff and we spent much time thinking and talking with one another about these issues.

There were times when the cultural differences were funny or poignant and all the participants enjoyed the differences. There were times we shared lovely sweet private exchanges with our culturally different new friends. Sometimes living together wasn't really so difficult, but it could be mighty fatiguing.

My love and respect for the ECUSA bishops and spouses was cemented over the Lambeth weeks. It was they who were accommodating, caring, and found the humor in such a difficult place. It was they who were modest, understated and held the conference together rather than encouraging a full-scale Episcopal riot. It was they who gave me the ability to notice the funny or ironic things and to allow the other stuff to slide away.

:ame to Lambeth to meet You in new friends
ns.

ᵣhysical needs were seen to, from more than
enough food to eat to portable loos playing classical
music.

Minds were stimulated and enhanced and challenged
through the gifts of varied presenters.

Blessings came to us in all sizes—young children—
teenagers—young, middle and older adults—all with
their own special style and grace!

Earth; this world became smaller and more known to
each of us as we traveled from country to country
through the stories of our brothers and sisters from
around the world.

Testaments, Old and New, were explored together during Bible study time. Listening, praying, sharing and
reading Scriptures together with God's help.

Hats on for the tea we had with the Queen at
Buckingham Palace—hats off to the Archbishop of Can-
terbury and Eileen Carey for the hospitality at Lambeth
Palace and the Old Palace at Canterbury.

Christ and His "Crowning Glory" were presented to us through drama and music—joyous, lively, quiet—by many and sometimes by only one.

Outings were provided for our relaxation and to widen our knowledge of this beautiful country—England.

Night time found beds that at first seemed too soft or too firm, becoming just right to revive us with much needed sleep.

Fasting, powerful mediations from Jean Vanier and the blessing of God's peace through quiet prayer and tearful reconciliation—we were fed.

Energy needed was given us in the daily Morning and Evening Prayer. Jesus' Body and Blood fed and renewed us in the daily Eucharists.

Religious orders and the chaplaincy team planned and prepared our worship services and were there to soothe the hurried, worried, harassed, and weary pilgrims.

English elves (as well as other elves from many other countries) everywhere: before we came, while we were visiting, visible and invisible. Their work not to be finished until long after we're gone.

Never, never, never will we be the same. Thank you God, for enriching and enlarging our knowledge of You and showing us the awesomeness of Your presence.

Courage we need as we go home and evangelize our countries. The truth shall set you free. This shall be our compass.

Eternal God reigns! As we leave Lambeth '98, the Spirit of God goes with us now and forever. Amen! Amen! Amen! Until we meet again.

I remember the first hours and days of the conference, registering, settling, greeting, wondering, and walking, as a blur. We located our assigned rooms and areas for meals, and the  strategically placed "luxury loos" around the campus. We learned to queue for the loos, for meals, for everything, without exception. The bishops found their sections and the plenary halls, and the spouses found their Bible study groups and the Spouses' Village—that splendid structure of white tents.

Attending Lambeth for bishops' spouses was so important to spouses that they rearranged their lives to participate. They found care providers for those with children or parents that they cared for in their daily lives. They kenneled their pets. There were some who resigned from their jobs. Others left loved ones, friends, family, children, in dangerous surroundings. We came as if drawn by a magnet—as if our very souls were being drawn together in some unexplainable way, by a powerful source. This drawing together created the essence and excitement of the Lambeth Conference and the Anglican Communion.

1998 marked the second Lambeth that included spouses as a part of the conference. They were invited by Eileen Carey, wife of the Archbishop of Canterbury, The Most Rev. George Carey. The 1998 Spouses' Program showed an increased strength—in number of spouses (nearly double), in offerings for spouses, in visibility of spouses, and in the five male spouses who participated. This was exemplified by the centralized location of the Spouses' Village in the midst of the Kent University Campus. In contrast, in 1988, an open tent was placed at St. Edmund's School which could only be accessed by climbing small fences and crossing fields. An interesting sight to watch! Actually, the climbing of fences was really the climbing of steps that went up and over the fence. The 1978 Lambeth did have programs for spouses but they were not held at the same location. Instead, there was a short conference for spouses but it was hard for many to attend as the programs were scattered throughout England.

The 1998 Program offered many opportunities for gathering together for worship, learning and fun. Offerings ran the gamut from airplane repair (a bishop's spouse in Australia flies her husband all over the vast expanse of the diocese) to repairing mitres, from an exploration of the theology of being a bishop's spouse to farming. There were day excursions to various places of spiritual importance and of fun. There were daily exercise and stress reduction offerings as well. Unfortunately, spouses were limited in what they could participate in due to seating or bus capacities.

For the entire community, there were the bishops' plenaries covering a myriad of issues and concerns such as world health and hunger. There were also evening programs that included a talk by Susan Howatch and an evening musical by the spouses which was great fun for all who participated or joined in the evening festivities. Once again, the ladies attending Lambeth donned their hats for a wonderful day which included a luncheon at Lambeth Palace where Prime Minister Tony Blair delivered a rousing, heart-felt speech to a somewhat intimidating group (Are there really 750 Bishops here?) which made his interest in the Church and State working together on social justice issues seem genuine and encouraging. He spoke on the world debt and issues surrounding it. Then it was off to Buckingham Palace for afternoon tea with Queen Elizabeth, Prince Phillip and Prince Andrew. The Purple Tea Party, as Queen Elizabeth called it, was a fine taste of pomp and circumstance. Dressed in purple cassocks and, of course, hats for the ladies, we awaited the royal entourage as we sipped tea, ate scrumptious and perfect looking delicacies, walked the immaculate gardens, and enjoyed the bands' music. Some exchanged a few words with Prince Andrew and Philip, offered Her Majesty a nod and a smile, and occasionally a hand, and enjoyed conversing with her Royal Guards. The day concluded with a slow and gentle boat trip down the Thames as the sun set.

By far, for most spouses attending Lambeth 1998, the most significant and formative experience was their daily Bible study groups. Here the spouses gathered in groups of about ten spouses for prayer, scripture, and reflection. There were spouses from around the globe in each of the groups. For those who did not speak English there were groups in French, Spanish, and other languages. Here the spouses gathered to share and break open God's word and to join in loving struggle to explore and embrace the word.

It is in these gatherings that encountering Christ in others occurred most deeply. A retired bishop's spouse who attended the 1978 and 1988 programs for spouses reflected on the impact Bible study had for her in the 1988 program.

> The small groups and Bible studies were certainly the highlight for me. I felt humbled and in awe of so many in other parts of the world who were either suffering themselves, or shared intimately with those who were. As we prayed together and grew to view each other as sisters in Christ, it became apparent that we would never be the same people we had been when we arrived. Life-changing? Yes, but what I sensed was soul work for all of us. We realized how differently we lived, what different expectations we faced, how our world views differed and yet we were united in Christ. In spite of our differences, we were one in the important basics of our faith. That seemed to me to be the direct action of the Holy Spirit at work within us, and one for which I shall always be grateful. I can not know what effect that experience had on others, but I do know that even ten years later and in retirement I remember those women and their stories. I look forward to being reunited with them at a future time. I also know that what we experienced *was* the church. We loved and accepted each other as we were, with all of our differences and in spite of those differences we knew we were united. That experience gives me hope for the church here where we share so much in culture and practice, and yet seem to think so differently.

The spouses program offered times for fun, for community, for learning, but it also offered times of challenge, times of difficulty in communicating and understanding. There was the ever-growing realization and experience of being with people who approached Christianity and scripture in very diverse ways. There were conflicting opinions on the issues Lambeth engaged and struggled with: Christian-Muslim relations, world debt, sexuality, the role of developed countries in responding to developing countries, interpreting the Bible, the role of bishops' spouses, to name some. And while only the bishops developed legislation and voted, the spouses were engaging the same issues with each other and with bishops. Our way of encountering the issues and each other was through story and not legislation. Some bishops were heard to comment that they envied the spouses as they seemed to have the more spiritual and theological experience.

> Some spouses at times experienced frustration. There was the feeling there was no "work" for us. That no one cares what the spouses think about the issues of the day. Granted—we were not elected. However, we do live with these issues daily the same as our spouses do. We suffer the slings and arrows that come with our spouses' position. We are committed to our faith, our Lord, our spouses. Otherwise we wouldn't be here, we couldn't do what we do, whatever that is, from doing the purple laundry to running diocesan organizations. As one spouse reflected: I didn't come to do crafts, however much fun

they are; I didn't come to listen to people tell me how wonderful spouses are in ministry. I am tired of hearing about the male Bishop spouses. Yes I am frustrated, but then I tell myself, let it go, enjoy, let somebody else solve the Church's problems. You're in England for three weeks and you're going to see the Queen.

The Good News was that God, acting in our lives at Lambeth, kept us together, both in small, intimate ways and in large, legislative ways. We all stayed at the table, giving and receiving, learning and listening, breaking bread and feeding one another, washing the feet of our neighbor and praying for forgiveness, and for challenging and being challenged by the Risen Christ and those we encountered. God was ever present. Thanks be to God!

The paths at the University of Kent, where Lambeth was held, are well embedded in our minds, our souls, and the soles of our feet. To get anywhere on the campus required extensive walking on paths. We walked and walked to get to worship, to Bible study, to eat, to workshops, to plenary sessions, and even to town. There were cement paths, rock paths, paved paths, grass paths, dirt paths. There were wide paths and those that were very narrow. There were the shortcuts across parking lots including those with raised squared grids that hurt one's feet. Sometimes there were even parallel paths—with one marked for bikes which was mostly ignored as the 2,000 plus participants walked their way through Lambeth. Walking on Lambeth paths was something we all shared. In fact, as time and the miles moved along, and our feet became tired and sore, our feet became a common topic for even the briefest of meetings.

During Lambeth, paths bound us together in common experience, just as Eucharist binds us together. In the three short weeks we journeyed many miles together, with people we knew and people we grew to know. There were people whose paths we crossed and others chosen to walk the path with us. At times the paths were crowded with everyone trying to get across campus at once or when people stopped to discuss an issue, argue about something, share a story, ask for help, or even pray together.

Christian pilgrimage is defined as "God's child making her way through this earthly world, and not, as society would have us believe, a child making her own way through this earthly world to God." This discovery changed preconceived ideas and attitudes, and removed unreal fears which allowed us to see we are on a common journey. We experienced evidence of this by the way our cultures began to complement one another; hearing and comprehension became clearer and we saw more similarities than differences.

We invite you to journey with us down some of the Lambeth paths as we tell our stories. Some will be easy paths, some more difficult. Some sweet and gentle and others challenging and rough. There will be side-trips down paths that branched off the ones we used daily. These are the stories of 33 spouses, including three male spouses, who walked the Lambeth paths for three weeks in the summer of 1998. They come from across the country and from every type of diocese. While you may not agree with what any specific one has to say, we hope you will walk with her (and in some cases him). It is in our stories that we can encounter the Anglican Communion and all that it struggles with and celebrates together. So put on some comfortable shoes and walk with us.

The campus of the University of Kent, Canterbury, has a paved walkway, a lifeline at the Lambeth Conference. It was the walking path from Parkwood, where many of us lived in two or three-coupled cottages, to Darwin, Eliot or Rutherford Hall which others of us called home. There were housed the dining halls and meeting rooms. From the most distant block of cottages to the farthest hall was over a mile walk.

One could not escape the path unless possessing a bicycle or car. Few did. Hall residents traversed the path to participate in the spouses' Bible study groups at Parkwood. All walked the path to the spouses' home tent for programs, to the Senate House for private prayer and meditation, to the enquiry office, the market place, plenary hall, and St. Columba and St. Augustine Hall for thrice-daily worship. We walked the path to special programs, to board motor coaches departing for spouses' excursions, for trips to Canterbury Cathedral, the Old Palace and London day. The path was our superhighway of connection to persons, events and corporate prayer.

We took the path to be fed by the Eucharist, by dining hall meals with old friends and new, by the extraordinary trust which developed among the members of the Bible study groups. The path from their doors to mine for our Bible study seemed long, they grumbled. The path was shorter by Lambeth's end, agreed my dear daily morning companions.

On the path were heard voices chattering, laughing, exchanging friendly greetings, accompanied by broad or shy smiles, reflecting our home worlds. The shoes, head coverings, red and blue Lambeth bags, recorded classical music playing as one strolled by the green "necessary" trailers, the view from the path by the home tent of the spire of Canterbury Cathedral nesting in the valley below. These images and recollections of sound quilt my patchwork memories.

The Lambeth path was variously a road to Emmaus, a wilderness journey, and always a walk with Paul as we daily studied 2 Corinthians. For all of us the Lambeth path was a walk with Christ. With anxiety, expectation and hope we embarked on a path. Each of us was the character Christian on the journey depicted in John Bunyan's *The Pilgrim's Progress.* We perhaps encountered hazards and our own "Slough of Despond." As the spouses observed the bishops, who were striding, tiptoeing or skipping along the path of discussion and mutual concern, I thought of Robert Frost's poem "The Road Not Taken," two paths, thus choices and implications.

What is clear to me is that we walked the path together at the University of Kent. We had to in order to get where we were going. We were seeking God's will and unity in Christ on the Lambeth walk. To walk the path was the way home.

Teach me thy way, O Lord, that I may *walk* in
thy truth;   —Psalms 86:11

    and I shall *walk* at liberty, for I have sought thy
    precepts.   —Psalms 119:45

for we *walk* by faith, not by sight
                            —2 Corinthians 5:7

    Each day at the Lambeth Conference we remem-
bered that to walk the path was the only way home.

I overheard someone at the conference say what a blessing the small Bible study groups were. They continued by saying, "wouldn't it be great if we could get to know everyone here in this kind of setting?" That is, getting to know a vastly different people from different cultures in a personal and confidential gathering. Here, in Bible study groups, we were able to make friends, share, laugh, cry, and celebrate on a personal level.

It seems that the value of the Bible study process is that it brings strangers together in a context that reminds them of their reason for being together: their response to and rootedness in the Good News of Jesus Christ. Each of us hears that news in a slightly (or dramatically) different way, but it all begins with our engagement with the person revealed in the text, who alone offers the possibility of loving one another despite those slight or dramatic differences.

At Lambeth, as the bishops' spouses gathered each morning for Bible study you could see the 630 spouses walking the pathways of the University of Kent, heading to different kitchens and groupings of chairs on lawns outside of kitchen doors. It was in these gatherings that the hearing of the Gospel in slightly (or dramatically) different places happened, and our views were engaged and explored. There were times of silence, of disagreement, of pain, of laughter. It was here that many warm tears of joy and sorrow were shared as we shared our stories.

> Lambeth was a beginning—traveling down a new road in my Christian journey. And probably the most nurturing encounters on the journey so far came during our daily Bible studies. We had all come from different experiences culturally but shared many of the same challenges.

Our Bible study groups wrestled with language barriers, marveled at social and political struggles experienced the world over, wept at many hardships and tragedies, admired each other's rich native histories, and became friends in spite of differing opinions. The Anglican Communion as experienced at Lambeth was a journey around the world on the pathways of Lambeth in the span of three weeks!

Our faith in Jesus and the guidance of the Holy Spirit created the link of "community and spirituality." These factors established a safe and secure environment where each bishop's spouse felt safe enough to share her Christian pilgrimage around the kitchen table.

For 22 hours over a three-week period, nine women met in a small room. We prayed together, read scripture, and shared stories. We came from Kenya and Tanzania, from the Yukon and the West Indies, the United States, Northern Ireland and England. What I remember most are the stories.

For one of us from Kenya, because there is so much sickness and death, Saturday has become a day for funerals—*every* Saturday. Once a day of rest or celebration, it is now one of sadness. And yet she exudes great faith and a quiet serenity. Her face stays with me—her wonderful smile—it lit up the room.

For another there was constant talk of the need for better education for the children in Tanzania. She implored us all daily to help. She remembers with fondness the dedication of the missionaries who once ran many schools, but they are now long gone—forced to leave.

Still another young woman from Tanzania spoke movingly of the sacrifice required of bishops and spouses. She described his frequent absences as a "deep wound" for the children. These women, especially in Africa, work closely with the Mothers' Union and other organizations to improve their lives. Often, the bishop is "Papa" to the flock, then these women are "Mama." They do not have a choice in this. Yet it is clear that, as women of faith, they try to live out their Christian calling.

For another of us, a story of persecution and incarceration in a prison camp in Cuba. This was a hard labor camp, and yet, out of the few precious minutes each day allowed to themselves, the Christians gathered together behind the latrines, formed a circle and prayed. She made it clear her faith was all that got her through that terrible time. She was separated from her husband who was also sent away, and from her young child. She spoke movingly of the rights we enjoy in the United States. Her words: "This freedom—it is a beautiful thing."

Before the conference ended, deadly bomb blasts went off at the US Embassies in both Kenya and Tanzania. And shortly thereafter, another bomb in Northern Ireland. How extraordinary that all these countries were represented in our one small group. I see all their faces. I carry them with me daily. Where are they now? What are they doing? What danger threatens them?

It was a kind and generous group. We did not always agree but we listened carefully and respectfully to one another. We allowed for differences between us. It was almost a physical space. And for me it has become holy space. I go back and revisit it. I strive to understand in a way I never would if we had spoken sharply to one another or pushed our point of view with a need to "win" the argument.

It felt like a transformative experience with Morning Prayer and Bible study the path to that transformation.

As clergy spouses, we have felt the pain our spouses have felt as they seek to proclaim the Gospel in an often alien and hostile world. We could share that with each other. And at Lambeth, in our Bible study groups, we were often able to listen and talk openly about the pain and division experience within Anglicanism and in our world. But we also discovered that we were one in Christ, and we could each pray for one another and for the wisdom, courage, and love to forgive and seek healing in our broken world. In diversity we found unity in Christ.

> In Bible study I experienced a growing fellow-ship with other spouses from very different areas. I'm the only person in my Bible study group from the mainland of the United States. This has pushed me to open myself to a wider inter-pretation of [God's] Vision! We spouses have gotten along better—and have been able to discuss sensitive issues (spousal abuse, homo-sexuality, etc.) in a much more honest, loving, and open way than has been reported by the bishops. A real treat at Bible study has been learn-ing songs from many different parts of the communion. In our humble kitchen meeting space, we have felt and sung "Wairua Tapu . . . , Wairua Tapu . . . Toms Mai" which means in Maori (a native language of New Zealand) "Holy Spirit, thou are welcome in this place."

The other nine women in my Bible Study Group became my international friends in Christ. We shared our stories and prayed together. In a brief time I became very aware that the most common factor that caused us to bond in our relationships was our common faith in Jesus Christ. Lambeth was the only experience I have ever had to meet people from all over the world, to pray together and to share our stories. There were stories of joy, but some of the stories were of poverty, hardship, and persecution. Always, though, the stories were told with expressions of thankfulness to a loving God for being present in the bad times, as well as in the good times. My Bible study group has pledged to pray for each other each Thursday, and I do that with great joy.

> For the first time in my life, I participated in a Bible study that really meant something to me— it turned into a wonderful forum for discussing issues of the day in a kindly, caring environment that could and did become heated. Where strong words were spoken and no common agreement was ever going to come. Where at the end of the conference those women that I thought were benighted and over the edge were as dear to me as the ones with whom I had no trouble agreeing on those difficult issues with which our husbands wrestled.

Prior to leaving for England, a lovely woman from Maine sent me a commentary on Second Corinthians knowing that I had been asked to be a spouses' Bible study group leader during

Lambeth. While I glanced over it, I prayed for my future study group with the hope that the Holy Spirit would guide our study with wisdom and truth. My group, as all others, was culturally diverse, represented a wide range of ages and interests, and all were committed to attending the study daily. What I had not anticipated was the exquisite bonding of friendship. In our scripture lessons Paul dealt with the developing church and the human problems of jealousy, isolation, power struggles, and the need for complete reliance on God for solutions. It was amazing how open and supportive our group became in such a short time.

As the group leader, I found myself spending hours every night in study and prayer wanting to present the very best that I could offer, but of course I always left the group after the morning time together feeling like I had received so much more from each of them. One particularly poignant moment was when our Nigerian spouse, Lucy, shared the difficulties she had to live through; she spoke of survival in her village, how difficult it was for mothers with babies and how some of these mothers would bring their babies to her. When that happened Lucy would give the mother all that she had.

The highlight of Lambeth for me was the early morning Bible study group I attended each day. My group included another American, a German Lutheran woman married to an English bishop, a woman from Australia, three African bishops' wives, and our leader, a Canadian. It was here on a daily basis that I felt the drawing of my soul to those very different, but equally precious women. We were at once prayerful, supportive, understanding, confiding, loving with a strength and depth that one seldom is privileged to experience. For me, Africa, Canada, Australia, Germany and England were brought alive; my eyes, heart and understanding were opened and enlarged in unimaginable ways. It was like jumping into a diamond and seeing the various dimensions which allow the light source to truly shine and enhance the stone. The light source in my Bible study group shone on the faces and through the hearts and minds of each woman there, enabling her story to be shared, heard, and understood, thus allowing our hearts to overlap with a new strength, love and understanding that could only have been possible because of the source which originally drew us together—The Holy Spirit.

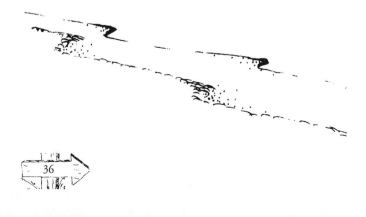

I walked as rapidly as possible for about a mile and a half in a completely unfamiliar place. I entered the room where my assigned Bible study group of bishops' spouses was meeting for the first time. I smiled and said, "good morning" to a group of eight women whose spouses were bishops in Pakistan, Uganda, Nigeria, South Africa, India, England and the United States. The leader of our group responded with, "You are late! You will not be late tomorrow." It would be an understatement to say that I was a bit startled by the greeting. Frankly, I wondered if I would be coming back "tomorrow."

I did return to the Bible study, but each day of that first week was painful. As we attempted to study Second Corinthians and to talk about implications for leadership, it seemed to me that we were as many miles apart in perspective as we were geographically.

My own personality and group experiences through the years have shaped me into a person who values process. Though this is time consuming, I prefer to listen to what each participant says and refrain from direct criticism of an expressed opinion. I began to feel quite outnumbered in this perspective. Actually there were times when I felt verbally attacked.

It seemed that most of these women interpreted and lived out their role as the bishop's wife in a very authoritarian manner. Most agreed that as the bishop's wife one was called to teach and admonish other women, including clergy wives, about how to live the Christian life. In the bishop's absence, they were called to speak for the bishop.

One day I gathered the courage to say, "I want you to know that I admire and respect your roles in your dioceses, but, quite frankly, it would be very inappropriate for me to speak for the bishop or to presume to tell anyone what to do because I am his wife." I tried to explain that I perceived my ministry as being one of love and presence in our diocese and my work with disabled preschool children in the public schools to be the way I lived out my call to ministry as the bishop's spouse.

After that day, I tried to walk at least part of the way back to my dorm with one of the women. Those walking visits were always blessings. I loved the time spent talking to them individually. We talked as sister Christians, wives, mothers, daughters, and friends. On my last day, it was hard to tell these women goodbye and I realized how thankful I was that I kept "going back."

Now, as I reflect on the experience, I realize that my decision to return each day was a gift of the Holy Spirit. I did not want to go back, but through the grace of God I did attend and participate in the daily sessions. I grew to appreciate how the hardships and dangers that so many of these women and their families faced daily influenced their attitudes and behavior. I grew to respect and admire their courage and willingness to assume leadership roles in very difficult and sometimes life-threatening situations.

I learned, once again, how my notion of the way to do things has been shaped by my culture. I learned, once again, and at a new and deeper level, that there is more than one way to do something. Ultimately, I experienced the power of our unity as Christians and Anglicans who were attempting to live a life in response to our Lord's call.

I am thankful that once again the doors and windows of my universe were opened. I am thankful for patience, love, and understanding that were gifts of the Spirit. I am thankful that once again I have grown and am a better, stronger Christian.

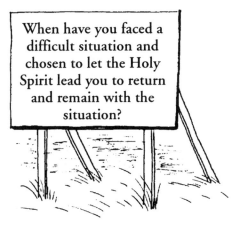

When have you faced a difficult situation and chosen to let the Holy Spirit lead you to return and remain with the situation?

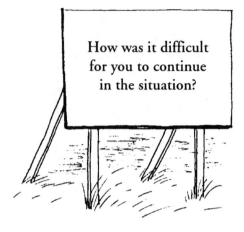

How was it difficult
for you to continue
in the situation?

What are you
thankful for and
what do you take
with you from
that situation?

"Alleluia"

The bishop earns a salary of $200 a year. He is always working. There is no privacy. People are constantly coming to the door for food, clothing, lodging. In addition to her own job as a high school French teacher, she cares for five of their own children and is foster mother to five others whose parents have been killed in the genocide. She is a Tutsi, her husband a Hutu whose brothers killed all her relatives because they were of the wrong tribe. Nonetheless, she's good to the murderers in his family. She prays for them and visits them regularly in prison. Why does she do this? Because she says she believes Jesus' words are true that one should love our enemies and pray for those who persecute us (Matthew 5:44). And that one cannot repay wrong with wrong but must do everything possible to live in peace with everybody (Romans 12:17-18).

This is just one variation of a theme that characterizes the lives of members of this bishops' spouses Bible study small group. I was a group leader of one of the Lambeth spouse program's two French/Swahili speaking groups. Our eleven members came from the Congo, Rwanda, Burundi, Kenya, Madagascar, and France. I was the only non-African member of the group. Professionally we were five teachers, an attorney, a physician, a writer. Among us we had 49 children. Most of the members spoke French, Swahili and a local language or English, Swahili and local language. Several bridged the French-English barrier by communicating with each other in Swahili or in Kirundi.

We began each session with prayers and songs in English, French, and Swahili. One Swahili song, "Nasema Asante" touched the Spirit so powerfully with its tuneful cadences that it didn't matter what language it was in, we all loved it. In the first week we started singing in French, English, and Swahili the song, "Praise to the Lord together singing 'Alleluia.'" By the end of the third week we had added verses in Kirundi, Malagasy, Kikuyu, and Kikamba. For the Bible study we broke into Fracophone and Anglophone subgroups and then came back together at the end for more singing and prayers.

All the women had experienced extreme poverty, and there was not one from Rwanda, the Congo, or Burundi who had not had friends and family killed in the genocide. They had personally witnessed pillages, rape, massacres of all kinds, babies being butchered out of their mothers' stomachs, and other unspeakable atrocities. They were housing children whose parents had been murdered and some were sheltering widows. The Congo (formally Zaire) should be one of the richest countries in the world, with fertile soil, vast mineral wealth, and a river whose force could provide enough electricity for the entire African continent, yet its 44 million people are among the poorest on earth. They have just emerged from 32 years of ethnic hatred, brutality, killings, chaos and misery under the harsh rule of the dictator, Joseph Mobutu. Mobutu is now dead but ethnic struggles began anew this summer.

The themes of Paul's Second Letter to the Corinthians, spoke with great clarity to our group. Forgiveness, mutual openness to God, being ambassadors for Christ, reconciliation, living justly, giving generously, finding hope and joy in serving Christ— these Gospel values have been tested again and again in the lives of the members of this group. And current events reminded us poignantly of the immediacy of the suffering. One morning Pascaline came in with the news that 129 people had been killed in her home diocese in the Congo. A week later, Josephine from Kenya gave us the first reports of the American embassy bombing in Nairobi. How real to us were Paul's words, "We are afflicted in every way, but not crushed; perplexed but not driven to despair; persecuted but not forsaken; struck down but not destroyed . . ." (2 Corinthians 4:8-9a).

I had requested a French speaking group because I knew that its members would come from some of the most challenging places on this planet and I had wanted to get a world view vastly different from my own. I got all of this and so much more. I had not expected to be bowled over by the profound, unshakable faith of our members; faith which had been so severely tested was a powerful witness to a God who suffers yet overcomes evil. They have put a human face on the tremendous sufferings of the African continent. The grim statistics now represent the friends and family of people I have come to know and to care about very much. These brave women are the embodiment of both the crucifixion and the resurrection of Jesus. As an American living my life and my faith and dealing with the issues I have to confront, my daily life seemed trivial and superficial in comparison. These women have a kind of courage I'd never witnessed before. Their sheer joy in the Gospel and their utter reliance on the God who upholds all humanity renewed my own sense of commitment and joy in the Lord. They rekindled the fire of my own faith. So for my very special sisters in this group and all that they taught me, every day I "Praise the Lord, singing 'Alleluia.'"

Where have you encountered world views different from your own?

As I listened to each bishop's spouse  introduce herself on the first day of Bible study, I quietly thanked God for giving me a group of women who could speak English. It was obvious that diminutive sari-clad Hepzi, wife of a bishop of the Church of South India, was not willing to try out her halting English very much, but she seemed to get the drift of what the rest of us were saying.

One day during the second week, as I was clearing up the cups and saucers after the study, Hepzi hung around. She wiped off the table, put away the milk, and helped me dry dishes until it was time to go to morning workshops. Clearly she had something on her mind. As we walked towards the center of the university she broached it.

"May I speak with you personally?" she said in painfully careful English.

"Of course," I replied, wondering if I had offended her somehow during the study that day.

"As I listened to your teaching, I felt God was saying I could ask you something." She paused, and I nodded encouragingly. Did she need money? I remembered that I had no English pounds left and only a small traveler's check.

"My son, Pradeep, wants to get his commercial pilot's license. He wants to go to flight school in America. Can you help us?" she asked softly.

I went into cautionary mode, knowing I had to have more information before I made any promises. "Hepzi, can't he get his license in India?"

"Maybe," she said, "But in flight school, students must pay for their fuel. In America, fuel costs so little it will make his education much less expensive. We have saved money for many years, and have $15,000. We may need more, but most of all we need a sponsor. He has been turned down for a visa three times."

I wondered why, but realized this was a conversation that could not be carried out while negotiating a rut-strewn footpath in single file. "Come with your husband and see us," I said. "Maybe we can help." In silence we upped our pace and made it to the workshops just in time.

Later that week, Hepzi and her husband came to see us. He explained that being a Christian meant Pradeep could not get government scholarship help in India, and might not be accepted at an Indian flight academy. American schools were less expensive, but American visas were difficult to obtain right now, because of Indian nuclear testing, which America disapproved of. The bottom line was that if Pradeep could get accepted at an American flight school, and have an American sponsor, he might be granted a visa. Would we sponsor him was the question.

Part of me did not want this responsibility. Another part of me rose to the challenge. "Can you get a list of flight schools in our diocese?" I asked. They looked at each other, tipped their heads from side to side in a typically Indian affirmative motion.

"OK," I said hopefully. "I'll see if we have any churches in those places that might want to sponsor an Indian student." We all began to get excited.

They phoned home to India and their son faxed them a list of schools which he thought were probably in our diocese. Two of them seemed promising. I e-mailed the rectors of neighboring parishes. Within a few hours both rectors had replied, expressing eagerness to sponsor Pradeep, and offering assurances of housing, financial help, and a supportive Christian community if he came to America. My husband wrote a letter to the consulate in Madras. It looked like we might be on our way down this new and unexpected path. With prayer, this thing just might happen.

It struck me that this is what it means to be part of a world-wide Christian communion: people in one place, to whom God has given much, helping people from another place who have needs. Because Hepzi and I had been placed in a group together, where bonding occurred and trust was formed, prayers were answered and family dreams were taken a step closer to realization.

With whom have you formed bonds where you have sought ways to share from your abundance?

I understood the pain of one who shared her story of having a profoundly disabled child in a developing world where there are few medical and governmental supports. I also had a profoundly disabled child, but our bishop got the state laws changed so we could get the support we needed. I was truly humbled to hear stories of great courage and sacrifice: the wife of a bishop whose election was contested and arbitrated in a civil court; those from Nigeria, Uganda, and India who lived where discrimination against Christians was constant and unending; one from the Republic of Ireland whose husband was actively condemning the violence in Northern Ireland in the face of great criticism; and from Australia one whose husband had publicly confronted the divisions within our own communion, but not without some price.

> Our interpretations of scripture were as diverse as our cultures. During some sessions we found ourselves at odds. However, we stuck together. I often pondered what it was that held us together. Was it the fellowship which filled a void—a void I had allowed to occur because of years of over-booked schedules, increased travel, and learning to cope with a new life style? The emptiness in my situation was a lack of "community and spirituality" caused by poor planning and role demands.

Sisters in the Lord

The tears came from somewhere that I had never known before. They poured silently and copiously down my face. They surprised me and I slipped out of the Bible study not wanting to disturb the opening prayers. When I returned after several minutes, I discovered the bishops' spouses from the US, Canada and Australia all weeping: I realized that my reaction to the vote on the resolution regarding human sexuality held the day before was not particular to me alone. I was afraid. Would our group be broken because of the powerful emotions present that day and because of the differently held perspectives?

The Bible study that I was attending was a program designed at Lambeth for all the bishops and spouses. Each morning for three weeks our small group of ten women would gather. It was a lovely picture to see the spouses all hurrying to classes held in the kitchens of our tiny graduate housing units. Open doors, laughter, greetings in different languages, and expectation filled the air. I, too, held an expectation. I wanted to learn just how Bible study could transform a group of people. Both here and at our General Convention we spend at least an hour each day devoted to small group Bible study. "For what ends?" I wondered. So I took notes in order to document what was happening among us.

The group I was in was truly a "hands around the globe" experience, with participants from Canada, US, England, Nigeria, Kenya, Uganda, North and South India and Australia. The text that Lambeth was to study was 2 Corinthians. Each day we prayed, read and discussed a passage. We were women who did not know each other and who knew even less about the diverse contexts in which we lived. Nonetheless, we faithfully shared our interpretations of the Bible and our life experiences over the three week long conference. During the opening session, the spouse from Nigeria addressed us as "Sisters in the Lord." What did that mean? Paul's second letter to the Corinthians led us on our way. I saw in the following passages that we discussed, examples of the ways in which scripture transformed us by illuminating our common "crushing" experiences as spouses, by expanding our different perspective on how we were "the aroma of Christ" and by challenging us to be God's "new creation."

2 Corinthians 1:8 "for we were so utterly, unbearably crushed . . ."

The question posed from this passage was, "What has crushed us as bishops' spouses?" An African bishop's wife told about how members of her diocese whispered to her to try and get her to change the way her husband was with people. He is a learned, shy person and people wanted from him an outgoing simplistic approach to things. She prayed and came to see the great complimentariness that they enjoyed as a couple. Her prayer led her to be more herself and to be able to rejoice and say, "This is me!" She could also watch over the years as her husband drew many young students into educational institutions. Another spouse shared her painful time when rumors about her husband's work were all around her. Confusion was the overriding feeling. We all discussed the nature of evil and acknowledged that as bishops' spouses we had a unique and intimate view of the capacity of the institutional Church to hurt and impede lives. Because the issues about which our spouses must speak out are very complicated, there is a lot of room for misunderstanding. People become anxious and confused. There is pain often directed as anger towards the bishop. We discussed antidotes to destructive forces and named the power of prayer to guide us through. Our human situations, although from very different cultures, showed us that we shared deeply a love of prayer. We began to know each other and trust our capacity to respect each other's lives. We explored our roles in being partnered with a bishop who was being asked to play out publicly some of life's most difficult questions. We all knew that prayer took the experience of being "crushed" and placed it firmly into God's hands.

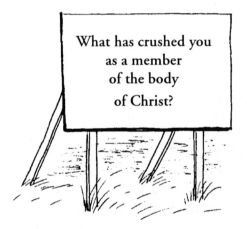

What has crushed you
as a member
of the body
of Christ?

2 Corinthians 1:15 "For we are the aroma of Christ to God among those who are being saved and among those who are perishing."

How were we "the aroma of Christ"? We learned about the oil wells in Nigeria, which bring great wealth to a few but never touch the poverty of the very people who live on the land itself. The anger of the poor is immense. Yet in this despair, the promises of the Gospel brought great joy to the people. They saw God as a God of miracles who gave them the hope of a better life. We from the US discussed the opposite problem, the dulling effects of great wealth. The aroma we hoped to emit was a call to a life where deeper values were presented in the Gospel accounts. From the vantage of our very different contexts, we shared the same commitment to the Gospel stories as invitations to an abundant life. We looked at our stressful experiences and saw the Bible as a resource for stability. We acknowledged our own love of scripture as a central to the faith of each one of us.

How were you "the aroma of Christ"?

2 Corinthians 5:17 "So if anyone is in Christ, there is a new creation: everything old has passed away; see everything has become new!"

How did our roles as bishops' spouses bring us the possibility of a new creation? The expectations of diocesan members of their bishop's spouse differ vastly. This is particularly true for the African wives. Their homes are open 24 hours a day. They must feed and house whoever comes to their door. They are in charge of all the women's activities, particularly The Mother's Union which is similar to our Episcopal Church Women (ECW). Nelias from Kenya told us of a time when she had no money for food. She had just one cup of milk left for her sick child. An old man came to her door and asked for a glass of milk. Nelias agonized and went off to pray. When she came back she poured him the milk and sent him on his way. Later that evening a friend, remembering the poverty of many of the clergy, showed up with two bottles of milk. She rejoiced in the abundance of her prayer! The opportunities given to bishops' spouses can in the midst of the challenges bring great joy and blessing. We all shared a call to lead lives faithful to the vows we took both at our baptisms and at our weddings. We knew many blessings in living out the several callings that each of us held at one and the same time.

How does your life as
a Christian bring
forth the possibility
of new creation?

These three sessions on 2 Corinthians were behind us as we met the day after the vote on human sexuality. My experience in Bible study that morning revealed to me how the work we had done together had in reality transformed us individually and as a group. We held very different points of view on human sexual practices because of the different contexts in which we lived. But we had built together a new creation where our common humanity and the environment in which it would thrive were given priority over difference and its ability to destroy. The foundation of this new creation was established while studying the Bible and allowing the Spirit to enlarge our capacity to accept the reality of another person as "the aroma of Christ to God." We had been shown the broad ground beneath our individual perspectives. So we proceeded in this session as we always had by listening to each other, holding hands and praying. Our common tears bound us as members of a Christian family who would not let each other go. We knew what it meant to be "sisters in the Lord."

How have you
been transformed
by your brothers
and sisters in
Christ?

Judith's Story I think it occurred early in the first week of our Bible study group. We had been listening to plenary sessions and the short 3-4 minute Bible study videos each day and then sharing our lives by answering the Bible study questions. We heard stories of trials and tribulations and about the great love and forgiveness God had commanded be shown the transgressors. I felt almost overwhelmed by the stories of faith and courage related to me by this group of women from around the world, particularly those who had faced persecution, hunger, death, and terrible uncertainty in their lives. We had listened to one of the group tell us how the Psalms had sustained her during the times of grief when two of her children died; another woman told of her absolute faith in God's goodness to heal her from blindness when the doctors told her she should probably seek the advice of her witch doctor if she wanted to see again. As well as what she told the doctor when her God did heal her! A long silence fell and I felt almost ashamed to speak. What could I possibly have to share. I had so much and I lived in a country with so much.

The silence began to stretch on into an uncomfortable interval, when Judith spoke up in a soft English accent and said, "Well, I almost hesitate to say anything, but I'm having trouble with my gardener." Was I hearing her right? Trouble with her gardener? Judith went on to tell us the story of how frustrated and irritated she had become with her gardener. He wasn't getting things done. He was doing the wrong things. He wasn't showing up at the proper times. The animosity had built to such a point she felt she just had to have it out with him. One day she looked out her window and saw him walking across the yard, his shoulders slumped, his head hanging down, and she realized there was some kind of problem. She went out and talked with him and asked if she could help. He relayed his story of troubles to her. She said all the anger and resentment seemed to melt away by the simple act of showing compassion. Judith went on to say that in the end it all came round to love and reconciliation. I realized that Judith's ordinary story about her trials with her gardener became extraordinary simply by its telling. Thanks to Judith I no longer felt I didn't have anything worthwhile to contribute. It made me understand that we all have a story to tell and we must learn to tell those stories. We must look to the ordinary that we do, and see it transformed to the extraordinary through God. We never know when we may have an opportunity to share our faith.

**Search your memories
of God's stories
within you and then
tell someone.**

Workshops

As spouses we had the fun and privilege of participating in creative workshops. One which I chose and enjoyed immensely was a painting class where we were asked to paint a self-portrait using a form of pointilism. This consisted of using a brush and making lots of colorful dots on the paper as we looked in a mirror and formed our image. Somehow from a distance these dots blended together and did indeed form our most interesting and varied portraits. The dots of color became more than simple dots of color—they formed beautiful images.

Lambeth was like going to church camp. We had things to do and places to be. I learned new skills like flower arranging and I could have gone to "Gentle Keep Fit" class if I had been ambitious enough to get there on time. I attended a seminar on health issues of children of the world, of particular interest to me in my work with international adoptions. For arts and crafts I can say I learned to make a mitre. My greatest learning, however, was not the finished product, but working side-by-side with others of different backgrounds and languages as we shared experiences, sewing expertise and assistance.

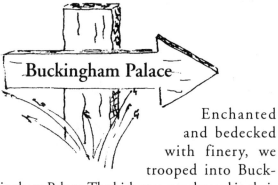

Buckingham Palace

Enchanted and bedecked with finery, we trooped into Buckingham Palace. The bishops were dressed in their Sunday best, this time their purple cassocks at Queen Elizabeth's request. The July afternoon was mostly sunny and pleasant enough for long sleeves. Excitement hummed in the air like static electricity before a storm.

> Our hats, infrequently worn or newly acquired, perched on our heads, fanciful calling cards for the gentle afternoon.

Framing the day was the pageantry: the royal footmen, Yeomen of the Guard, the bands of the Coldstream Guards and the Queen's Division (Normandy) playing "God Save the Queen" as she stood on the terrace before walking about to greet her guests. Broadway show tunes accompanying her stroll. The tea tents had lavish buffets of dainty sandwiches, luscious sweets, ice cream and iced coffee. There were tables and chairs on the lawn to help us enjoy the feast of tastes, sounds and colors. We admired the elegant outfits of bishops' wives from all over the world, especially the gorgeous hats, and pinched ourselves at being there.

Path's rejoining
Did you see the Queen? Did you get to shake her hand? What is she like?

These were the questions most frequently asked of me after returning from Lambeth. I smile and answer, "yes" we saw the Queen. "No" we were not one of the many who did actually speak to her and shake her hand but she is a lovely, gracious and very real person. My lasting feeling of the experience of having been invited to tea at Buckingham Palace was actually watching the interchange of Abigal and Paul when they met and talked with Queen Elizabeth. Abigal was in my Bible study group and we had become friends. She and her husband are from the Province of Canada and he is the Bishop of the Diocese of The Arctic. They are Eskimos and were wearing their native dress for the tea. Eventually they were selected to be in a group which the Queen would approach. I could see the broad smiles and excitement on their faces. When Queen Elizabeth did move toward them I heard her ask with enthusiasm, "Oh, hello, and where exactly are you from?" When Abigal and Paul answered, "We are from Iqaluit, in the Northwest Territory," the Queen's face just lit up. She reached out in excitement and held Abigal's arm exclaiming, "Oh, that is wonderful, I've been there! I remember visiting for the dedication of your cathedral over 10 years ago." The genuine pleasure this brought to Abigal and her husband who had traveled countless thousands of miles and many days and hours on planes to attend this Lambeth Conference, radiated from them.

Fifteen years ago when a seminarian from our diocese invited a young couple from Kenya to spend their summer at our youth camp, they came with gifts of the Spirit (Kenyan style!) to share with the adults and children who came to camp that summer, including my own. Sporadic contact was maintained over the years, but not once did we actually see one another until Lambeth 1998.

We knew that Joseph had become a bishop in Kenya and we hoped to see him and his wife while we were all in Canterbury. However, with so many participants at this Lambeth, just becoming oriented to the campus and the schedule was daunting! Several days passed, and still we had not seen them.

Midway during Lambeth was our big day in London with lunch at Lambeth Palace, tea at Buckingham Palace, and an excursion on the River Thames. While enjoying a spot of tea in the Queen's gardens, we asked another Kenyan bishop about our friends. He said, "They are right over there!" So it was in the middle of over 2,000 guests from around the world, that the world came together, with long and loving embraces between Kenyans and Americans!

Our first visit in fifteen years was thousands of miles from either of our homes and in the Queen's backyard! Suddenly, where we were meant little. Only hearing and learning from one another was important. The rest of our time at Buckingham was spent in conversation with one another. As light rain began to fall we remained focused upon one another, hearing about our lives, our hopes and dreams, our families, our work. Though literally worlds apart in many ways, the love and joy we shared in seeing one another again transcended and made small the differences in attitude or belief which are between us.

Crowning Glory

The culmination of three weeks' singing, dancing and costume-creation took centre-stage at the Lambeth conference on the final Thursday night with the performance of "Crowning Glory," a musical presented by members of the spouses' programme.

It began with dancing in the aisles and hoots of delight as cast members enticed the seated into a stream of song and movement undulating through the aisles. It ended with popping flashbulbs, standing ovations and shouts of "Bravo!" "Bravo!" [adapted from a press release by Katie Sherrod and Nan Cobbey, Lambeth Conference/Anglican Communion Office]

Turning in a kaleidoscopic circle of people, prayers, palaces, and meetings, was for this Lambeth "pilgrim" a joyous, soul touching drama. "Crowning Glory" was a parable, based on an Oscar Wilde short story, written and directed by English spouse Veronica Bennetts.

The music transcended language, ethnic and national barriers as we rehearsed with great glee and affection for one another. Presenting "Crowning Glory" as our gift to the Lambeth Conference on the Feast of the Transfiguration was indeed a high peak for me. Quoting from the finale—"We will travel with the music—we will reach the morning and our journey's end!"

Mari Hampton

St. James Palace

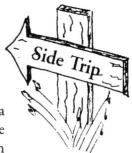

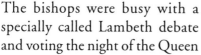

The bishops were busy with a
specially called Lambeth debate
and voting the night of the Queen
Mum's reception for all the dioceses with Church Army
programs. Therefore, many of the bishops were not
present for the trip to St. James Palace in London. Now,
I am a rather strong extrovert, but that night I was
developing the overwhelming feeling of "I really do not
want to be here; why did I come?" The reason I did
come was to honor the work of the Church Army in my
diocese, but it did not help much with the feeling of "I
know only a couple of people, so why am I here?"

I urged myself to wander about the room and get
introduced to the ECUSA Church Army leaders and to
mingle. As I did, I got the image of the Queen Mum
herself and how she had to rise to a role that she had not
chosen. Queen Mother Elizabeth married a prince and
had a comfortable, quiet life when a major change was
thrust on her and her family by the abdication of King
Edward VIII.

This woman, in whose home I was visiting, had
risen to many challenges life had presented to her during
her 98 years. She moved from wife of a prince to wife of
the King and then to mother of the Queen. She stayed
in London with her family and the people of London
during World War II, being a support and a symbol to
all she encountered.

As I watched her move through both large reception rooms, greeting and chatting with the people, I thought, "If she could do that all these years, and even now be totally present to each and every person she met, I could do my best to do likewise."

The Queen Mum has been a long time patron of the Church Army, which was established to enable ordinary men and women to share the Christian faith in words and action. Little did I know that I would be a beneficiary of Elizabeth's witness and sharing on an evening when I was feeling vulnerable and out of place. Grace happens even in the most sumptuous surroundings and sometimes when you least expect it. I pray that I may be faithful in modeling myself after the Lord who has been and remains worthy of our trust and is with us always even when we are feeling uncomfortable and alone.

How can you be
totally present to
each and every
person you meet?

Lambeth? What about it? Did I know what I was getting into? Would it be a meaningful event or would it be three weeks of "being a bishop's wife and waving a diocesan flag? Could I find a group of American wives to hang out with and avoid having to try to communicate with people I didn't know or understand? Which of the Shakespearen plays would Lambeth most resemble—"The Tempest" or "Much Ado About Nothing"?

Three weeks in England is a definite benefit for many of us. Three weeks of actually having meals and some time together with our spouses was a real benefit to lots of us. Three weeks of having to be in constant contact with people from all over the world was a benefit for all of us whether we could admit it or not. It's hard being civil and nice for that long! It is doubly hard for us westerners to be faced with the fact that our lives are cakewalks compared with two-thirds of our brethren in the world. Walking, talking with witnesses to atrocities and persecution that we can hardly imagine are constant challenges to us—living with them for three weeks makes us think too hard about things which we would really rather not think about. So far "The Tempest" is winning. Diocesan flags don't mean much here either—except as signs that we will align ourselves one diocese to another as a means of aiding our less fortunate sisters and brothers. Better trash those egos, too. No room at the inn for them. Dirty hands and emptying check books ought to be the order of the day here—and at home. Pretty vestments and processions are fun, but when we go to Lambeth Palace and Buckingham Palace and there are people wearing rubber thongs, I am suddenly rather ashamed of the angst I expended over my hat.

> We need to be responsible about giving money. We might think of the poverty and health problems in our own country which seem so hard to solve. Compared to the third world problems, ours are small.

Lambeth was like a giant, awesome, international family reunion. Differences in dress, language and life styles made me constantly aware of how enormous and diverse our Anglican Communion is. Yet, there were also frequent reminders of how our lives continue to touch one another.

> I was astonished with the different information, the alien views, given or not given, the different cultural contexts and life contexts on the part of many of the third world bishops and the naiveté of many. "Forgive our debts." "Don't touch a homosexual . . . it is contagious, you know!"

On the night after the final Lambeth Eucharist, we gathered together for a delightful picnic in and around the Lambeth Spouses' Village overlooking the city of Canterbury and the

Canterbury Cathedral. As dusk settled in, there came a spectacular, elaborate, and brilliant display of fireworks—incredible bursts of color and energy and celebration propelling us to go back out into the world and to live and teach the Gospel! Yet even in this, our diversity was present as some people who did not understand fireworks and had never experienced them hid in fear of the falling fire.

> At Lambeth, we were immediately immersed in the reality of our diversity. We worshiped, sang with, laughed and frolicked with, ate with, shared housing with, cried with, debated with, worked with, disagreed with, traveled with people very different from us in almost every way imaginable—color, language, sex, dress, beliefs, practices, ways of thinking, ways of living, to name just a few. Threatening and uncomfortable as these differences may have seemed at times, I believe they made us more whole, richer, and more God-centered in our focus. It was in our worship and prayer together and in our small Bible study groups that these differences were transcended by a filling of God's Spirit among us—where we could enter into each other's joys and sorrows—where the suffering and pain of many were expressed and heard. We were truly able to appreciate one another in these intimate times of sharing.

For me, of course, the most interesting part of Lambeth was the people we met from around the world. There was Teresa from Cuba whose son had gone to Spain for his first year of college. He was coming home for the summer and she had gone to the airport to meet him. She could see him through the glass, but the authorities would not let him enter. He had to get back on the plane and return to Spain. She could see him but not touch him. Then there was Alice from Kenya who was searching for her spiritual identity. Her role is clearly defined because much is expected from the bishop's spouse. They have to have their house open and available at all times. Many people come there, some sleeping on the floor. She must also travel with her husband and is called the mother of the diocese. She does not have any time for herself. Others echoed similar stories of having to let go of raising their own children so they could fulfill their responsibilities as mother in the diocese.

> I wrestled with my frustrations and anger that countries with so many natural resources cry poor and need so much aid, when they are killing each other and can't manage to govern themselves. They seem to be on the dole. They seem to be critical of us, but wanting our dollars. Confusing!

I am thankful for our freedom of religion.

> Meeting with and getting to know people from all over the world will change the way I read newspapers. Stories that before were about distant places I have never been, now will come alive with the faces of people I know who live there. We shared much about our homelands. We didn't agree on every issue, but we listened to and learned from each other and parted

friends. In other words, we fulfilled what I understood to be the spirit of Lambeth. My big disappointment was that many of the bishops did not conduct themselves in this same spirit. Rather, politics and parliamentary procedures seemed to abound.

The liturgies were remarkable; so different, yet so familiar. Those were some of the best times. Once one learned to be selective in the homilies one actually listened to, the services were a haven. That is the amazing thing about being an Anglican. We are so diverse with such different worries and such disparate lives. Yet together we are of one Lord, one faith, one baptism. We are many, but one in Christ. We are uneven, bumpy, multi-cultural Anglicans.

Each morning Eucharist and Evening Prayer was unique, indeed. New Guinea's fascinating Pidgin English kept us tongue-tied and grinning. Praying the Lord's Prayer together in our native languages was quite moving. Passing the Peace Polynesian style was a great favorite as we pressed noses and breathed in each other's spirit. As different and varied as we were, the common ground of our faith through worship was a powerful witness to our great Communion.

Bell Harry Tower

During the Lambeth Conference, on a free evening, one of the members of my Bible study group visited Canterbury Cathedral and had the opportunity to climb to the top of the Bell Harry Tower. As she was coming down, she prayed for each of us in the Bible study and as she was praying she realized that the tower was held up, not by braces or buttresses or interior reinforcing, but by the tension of the stones with each other. The tension has held that tower up a long time. When she told that story I thought how appropriate. There we were, representatives of the Anglican Church from all over the world, from different traditions, different experiences, different ways of expressing our beliefs. At the conference we were living with the tension of those differences and some wondered if we would be able to stay together as a church. However, it is the tensions between us that hold us together; we are like the stones in the Bell Harry Tower. Learning to live with our differences makes us strong. Treating each other with respect as we share our understanding of the Gospel is our witness to the rest of the world.

Lambeth transformed me. It opened my eyes to the dignity, intelligence, courage, and endurance of others. It gave faces to difficulties in the Sudan, Burma,

Cambodia, Iran, Ireland, Rwanda, and many other places. I have prayed for troubled situations but now I pray for people. People with intelligence and dignity and beauty. When I think back on my Lambeth experience I remember with joy my Bible study group: the laughter we shared, the singing, the stories and the wisdom of experience reflected through the Scriptures. I think of going on outings with Mary, my housemate from Bangladesh, grateful to have a partner. She and I also shared time in the sacred spaces set aside for meditation. And we often went to worship and meals together, waiting for our husbands.

Jesus said, "The glory that you have given me I have given them, so that they may be one as we are one, I in them and you in me, that they may become one, so that the world may know that you have sent me and have loved them even as you have loved me" (John 17:22-23). We are meant to practice living together in harmony, bringing the songs we sing individually and blending them to make a melody for God.

During the conference we celebrated the Feast of the Transfiguration. It was the anniversary of dropping the atomic bomb on Hiroshima. The Holy Catholic Church in Japan celebrated the Eucharist that day. The Nippon Sei Ko Kai apologized and asked forgiveness for their part in Japan's actions in World War Two. In the evening the spouses put on a musical production, "Crowning Glory," a parable of transfiguration, showing how we can all be transformed. "See the light is growing . . . feel the morning in you, you will never be the same." Wherever we are, whatever our experience, we are never the same when we allow Jesus to come into our lives. He is the one who transforms us. He was there at the conference. I saw him in the eyes and faces of people from all over the world.

When I got home and began visiting churches across the diocese, people told me they had prayed for me. "It was so good to have the *Anglican Cycle of Prayer*," one said, "because I could pray for you and for the conference every day." And another said, "I visited Canterbury with my daughter, so when I prayed for you I could picture what it was like. I prayed for you every day."

And then I knew why it was such a good experience for me, why I felt unselfconscious and able to reach out to others. It was prayers of friends back home, prayers of people from all over the world who held us together. We Anglicans will stick together just like the stones in Canterbury Cathedral. It takes work: forgiveness and reconciliation, listening to each other, speaking the truth in love. Lots of times we have to repair damage done when the forces of evil take over. We still live in a broken and hurting world. We are still imperfect people. But if we let Him, Jesus will transform us into whole and holy ones and He will keep the church as One.

How are you being called by our God to be an instrument of his reconciling love?

Home

On Leaving Lambeth

As we pack our suitcases
What shall we take with us?
Papers, books and photographs?
No, dear Lord, these are not the finest treasures.
From your sturdy vine
New branches flower with friendship
With the fragrance of living among other people
Who dwell on this earth you formed.

You nourish our growth on your vine
Surrounding us with song and prayer,
Sustaining us with your Holy Word,
Guiding us when we disagree,
Laughing with us when we play,
Filling us with new understanding,
Making us want to work for a world
That knows no hunger or disease,
That proclaims you are the Christ
The way, the truth and the light.

As we pack our suitcases
We gather the branches from one another
Carrying them into our own countries
To our families and neighbors far away.

Lord, thank you for the privilege of being in this place.
Come home with us.

Unfortunately, for me much of my Lambeth experience got rather buried in the ensuing onslaught of anger which we had to face once we got home—the result of the American participation in the famous vote. And we're still dealing with it. However, the smoke's clearing and I am sorting out my own experiences—and our busy lives go on.

> I believe I am a different person for having had this Lambeth experience. I am somehow enhanced and living in a larger dimension than I was prior to it. God has gifted me with a deeper awareness of His creation, presence, acceptance, and love of all His children throughout the world. I feel called to develop a wider understanding of His beloved and diverse people—especially those who are different from me in my tiny corner of the world. Our diversity in the Anglican Communion is so rich and colorful with varying hues and energy and sounds to celebrate and appreciate. This celebration touches something very deep within us—something that evokes God-consciousness.

The kaleidoscope of Lambeth continues to entertain, haunt, and convict me with vibrant colors and patterns. I give thanks for it! I may never see the whole picture, but I pray that I might grow in my generosity of spirit and somehow reflect many of the colors of God's love in my life and in my relationships with His children.

As we washed one another's feet in the ritual of foot-washing, I felt humbled and very aware of my humanity, while at the same time very aware of my oneness in Christ with these brothers and sisters whose feet had trod such varying pathways, all seeking God's love and bearing that love in unique and unexpected ways. These feet have all returned to the soil of homelands all over this world. Some are stepping on accelerators of modern cars; others are pedaling bicycles; others are making their way through the rough bush—all transformed in some way by this Lambeth experience.

> Through the sharing of our stories at Bible study, over meals, in our many queues, on buses, and as we walked the many paths, I was made more sensitive to the wide gaps between the "haves" and the "have nots" of the world. This heightened awareness came through the very sharing of our stories. These stories have changed me. For example, one change is the way I now read the newspaper. When the name of a country of a person I met at Lambeth appears, I am more attentive and read it more carefully. I hope now to look for ways the Church can respond more compassionately to the needs of the world.

I came home interested in Phoebe Griswold's presentation in which she talked of being a bishop's spouse as a theological journey rather than a spiritual one. It left me asking, "Just who is God for me?" I am still digesting.

The friendships formed and experiences we shared will forever change how I read the newspaper, how I watch the news of television, and how I pray the *Anglican Cycle of Prayer.*

> I know that I can never read a newspaper, or hear about persecution around the world, without attaching a face, a real person, to those events— whatever they may be. My daily prayer list has increased greatly. I'm also confident that there are people scattered around the globe who, because of three weeks together, are praying for me. The world has become smaller in important ways, and who my neighbor is has taken on new significance for me!

How do we reach out to God's children?

How might you include the news in your prayers?

We came to Lambeth and brought to the Communion Table our questions, our needs, our hopes. We left it not with so many answers, but with an understanding of the questions, not with every need being met but with those needs being heard, and as we looked on the faces of our brothers and sisters, our hopes were indeed answered in love.

> So, what about Lambeth? It was about people. It was great! It was about a shared and common faith. It was about breaking bread together. It was about sharing stories. It was about walking a common path. It was sad and wonderful at the same time. There are people like me, like us out there. It was great and I can't wait to go again. But, first, I have to rest up!

I pray that one of the lasting impacts of Lambeth will be reconciliation on an ever-deepening level. It was a powerful example to all present at the Lambeth Conference Eucharist when we heard the Japanese Church take ownership of their role (participation and/or omission) in the atrocities perpetrated on the Chinese people during World War II. This action touched my soul. We are all affected by reconciliation in our own life, whether it is with a spouse or child or sibling or friend after a misunderstanding or a time of distance from one another. We have heard about that which God has facilitated in the work of South Africa's racial reconciliation after apartheid. Sometimes reconciliation begins unintentionally as with the Swiss banks' opportunity to return bank funds to the Jews of the

Nazi holocaust when bank records were "found" in the shredder room. I can not help thinking that disclosure helped lead to the reimbursement of the Nazis' slave laborers in the Volkswagen factories. In attending the Church Army reception at St. James' Palace, I met a couple who told me of a group of Christians who were walking through the Muslim world of the crusades, going from village to village to apologize for the Christian domination in the name of our loving God! Why had I not heard of that before? The world should know about this! God leads us to reconciliation repeatedly in our lives. The Bible is filled with many stories of reconciliation. We have received a mandate from the Lord of the universe to respond honestly, without our usual self-protective and face-saving stance, to reach out to one another with open hearts and hands.

Lambeth was and continues to be an opportunity for reconciliation.

How do we
communicate
Godly things
together?

How are you called
to reach out to
others in the name
of our Triune God?

Leaving Lambeth

Like hillside fireworks,
Roman candles launched by God,
We dazzle with hope.

Contributors

Elizabeth Allan	Atlanta
Katherine Bainbridge	Idaho
Barbara S. Borsch	Los Angeles
Peggy Brown Buchanan	West Missouri
Mary "Carter" Coleman	West Tennessee
Betty Creighton	Central Pennsylvania
Nara Denar Duncan	Pittsburgh
Sally Fairfield	North Dakota
Chris Folwell	Central Florida (retired)
Sarah L. Grew	Ohio
Phoebe W. Griswold	Presiding Bishop's spouse
Mari Hampton	Minnesota
Elizabeth A. Hart	Southern Virginia
Karen E. Howe	Central Florida
Mary B. Howe	West Missouri
Jerrie Jacobus	Fond du Lac
Joan Jecko	Florida
Gretchen B. Kimsey	Eastern Oregon
Jane M. Lamb	North Carolina
Ira Pauline Leidel	Eastern Michigan
Mac McLeod	Vermont
Rebecca A. Parsley	Alabama
Barbara K. Payne	Texas

Mariann Price	Southern Ohio
Philip Roskam	New York
Dr. Anne Rowthorn	American Churches in Europe
Mary Carol Shahan	Arizona
Karen Sisk	New York
Diane Stanton	Dallas
Jan Wantland	Eau Claire
Larry Waynick	Indianapolis
Wendy Wimberly	Lexington
Ann Winterrowd	Colorado